112B Riverside Walk

This book is a work of fiction. Any references to historical events, real people or real paces are used fictitiously. Other names, characters, places and events are products of the author's imagination. And any resemblance to actual events or places or persons, living or dead is entirely coincidental.

Contents

112B Riverside Walk

Suicide

It was time to climb over the balcony rail and take a moment to consider my future, or maybe what was left of it. The welcoming downstream current stretched out far below me with its shimmering green water inviting me in. I couldn't swim that well these days, but I was convinced that the fall would kill me anyway.

It was with a certain regret that I uttered my last words. "Good bye world, I have to go and

leave you all behind."
The impact of the fall had knocked me senseless. It felt like choking at first, then shortly afterwards the suffocation started to get its grip on my throat as I fought against trying to save myself once again. There were some frantic attempts to struggle to the surface as my common sense slowly returned, but this is not what I wanted, or indeed needed to complete the stupidest idea I'd had for a long time. Why was it so silly? It started out okay as the solution to everything.

It was silent down here with the greenish brown water. The noise of bubbles rising along with flashes of light from the surface as I was spun round and round by that forceful current which was slowly dragging me towards the weir and a certain quick end. It really was the end of the line to do something like this in the first place and I knew it. I had reached this point of no return because of my misunderstanding of life and all of its consequences.

My determination to end it all was well advanced as I was taken down by the current and dragged along the bottom of the river. Gone were the sympathetic days of my normal understanding. Here was the answer to it all, a tidy end. Not for me the messy aftermath of a gunshot wound, or the neck cringing pain of a hanging. My friends and relatives wouldn't be tormented by my remains that needed to be tidied up afterwards.

And so it was that I had finally reached my decision to end it all on this glorious spring morning. It took for ages to reach the point of no return, I just had to hang on for a few more minutes and it would be done. Peace, calm and quiet at last, the very thing I had craved so long for. Just to get rid of the tormentors and interferers of this world and to leave me alone for once, was my only desire as I felt myself letting go of reality and drifting off to my new place of residence.

I was a god fearing man, but only in a casual way and only when it suited me to think that way. The colours of the water were by now starting to fade with every second, the buzzing in my head was reaching fever pitch as I had at last started to relax my grip on life as I knew it. Flashes of light

were no longer viewed through my eyes, but were inside my head as if someone was switching the lights on and off.
My need for air was at last a thing of the past. I was by now floating along in the current and enjoying it. My mind had gone numb with the cold as I felt some of the water enter my nose and throat. A final struggle with my arms to reach the surface and perhaps save myself had me smiling to myself, it was a pointless exercise and I had at last succumbed to my destiny.

I suddenly felt the hardness of the ground pressing into my back as whoever it was pumped my chest mercilessly shouting my name and slapping my face. I knew what they were doing so I just relaxed and let go, but they were too persistent and I could feel myself coming back. I tried to ignore them and hold my breath, but to no avail. It would seem that life wanted to return to my body against my better judgement.
'Interfering sods,' I thought as I coughed back into life. 'Why don't they leave me alone and let me get on with it.' "Come on Jack keep coming back you're nearly there." I heard one say as he crushed my chest into my back.

On opening my eyes I knew exactly where I was and it wasn't for me the place I expected. A large crowd of strangers had formed a circle around me and were peering down with excited expectations hoping for the worst. They were taking a particular interest in my progress as Charlie smashed again at my chest with those heavy hands of his. Jim organised the crowd with his continuous relaying of instructions and false information. "Right people, it's all over, my pal Jack just fell in the river and he's fine now, maybe just a little shook up, but no other problems. I will get the van along here Charlie and we can get him back to the apartment."

I was duly placed with a bump unceremoniously inside the van and the doors slammed shut to keep those nosy sods eyes from their constant expectant gaze.

"How are we going to get him into the apartment without that porter twigging onto what's happened, if he finds out the whole world will know by this afternoon Charlie."
"You just drive Jim and let me do the thinking."
We eventually arrived outside of the apartment

building with little ceremony and parked up on the grass verge. “Right Jim here’s the plan, Jack got pissed and fell in the river that should do it. It wouldn’t be the first time that Jack has returned home a few sheets to the wind, now is it?”
“Okay good idea, now let’s get him lifted out and we can stand him up and carry him in between us just like old mates returning from a party.”

The entry code was inserted into the shiny bright box and a slight click from the mechanism had the three of us moving inside the entrance hall and silently along past the porter’s window. “Hello boys, been swimming have we, or is it something more serious than that? Jack looks in a bad way, let me get some help.” The porter was a new guy and couldn’t do enough in his overzealous way, not that it helped our situation much as this was to be an undercover operation, or so we thought. Charlie was in there very quickly. “Listen mate whatever your name is, we are fine and just returning from an early morning party when our buddy here had a little mishap balancing along the railings, that’s all. We don’t need any help other than the key to his front door as Jack went out and forgot his.”

"My name by the way is Barnaby Wilks, I will take you up and open the door as you look as if you could do with some assistance."

"Don't worry about things like that, we can manage, give me the key here, we don't need any help thank you!" Charlie was incensed at this little bugger's insistence. The boys then got me into the lift and very soon afterwards I was stripped of my wet clothes and tucked into bed with a couple of hot water bottles.

So here we are, my friends Jim Sheen and Mad Charlie Watts. Charlie was a big man of advancing years with greying hair and a bushy out of control beard which he would constantly stroke back into position. This action was particularly noticeable when he was thinking. A very brusque man with a, couldn't care less attitude for this world. If mad Charlie couldn't get the answer to something he would just throw his arms around and say. "It will be all right in the end!" His visual appearance was that of a mountain man.

While on the other hand Jim Sheen was completely the opposite, a quiet sort of person of slight build with a rounded face that had a permanent smile etched across it, his fair hair was always kept tidy. Not the sort to mix with the likes of Charlie, he was very thoughtful and could sort out the answers to problems well before they arrived. He was a bit of a ladies man, but we didn't hold that against him.

So there you have it, my mates from when we were kids at school had rescued me from a watery grave and were in full attendance looking after me. "Here's a cup of tea Jack, hold on tight we will move your bed into the front room so you can look out over the river, me and Charlie have to go now.

Will you be okay for a couple of hours while we get to the betting shop and lay a few bets on?" "I'll be fine boys and thanks for this morning, promise me you won't mention any of this too Rosy as she wouldn't be able to handle it. What with me trying to end it all without even so much as a word in her ear."

"You just stay in bed until we return, that's all you have to do and nothing else, promise?" "Yeah no worries, just get that bottle of red from the fridge before you leave me stranded." At last I had come to the sensible reasoning of a balanced person and not a moment too soon.

Realisation at last

My name is Jack Sparrow, a very private person or so I thought. 'Deceased?' Well not quite. You see someone else thought for me in my last moments as my mind was in turmoil. The whole bloody thing had taken me over in one form or other and the inevitable end was not for me this time. I had friends that did the thinking for me at my last moments and they had brought me back from that other place.
It would take some time for the chest bruising to clear up, along with those pains in my head, but other than that I was fine and had regained my senses at last. My friends had made me promise not to go there again and I firmly agreed to refrain from anymore of the silly nonsense without speaking to them first.

It was easy to say, but at the time too difficult for them to comprehend as they had not been down that dark tunnel of despair to where there was no reason of any kind. I had been cast into that bottomless pit, devoid of all reason and logic.

I now have a deeper understanding of life without hope. I had at the time arrived in the dark place of despair and lostness.
That's where I had found myself.

My new residence is a waterside high rise apartment from where I could survey all of the movements along the riverside footpath from my balcony's lofty perch. The coming and goings of the drifters along with the undesirables of this world as they plied their trade between destinations.

The drug dealers were easy to spot, always on the lookout with furtive peaks behind them as they traversed the riverside walk. The river being a valuable resource for quickly disposing of any unwanted items at the merest sight of the police. There was also Dolly and her mate Gloria plus a few more on the game picking up tricks along the riverside after dark. It was a highway of dysfunctional misfits to say the least.

It had all been an accident me becoming involved in things that were not of my doing. Some said it was my nose for a story. Others said that I had been handpicked from those ordinary citizens that hated the injustices of this world, who knows. In the interim I had made lots of friends and enemies alike? Take that Brenda Jones for instance, she works in the Riverside Cafe, she was Barry Jones before her sex-change and we used to go to school together.

No more than a normal kid in those days and a good mate as well, but there lies the rub. She now thinks of herself as something special. She would rearrange her new chest with the inside of her arm at the same time as pursing her lips at any mention of how pretty she looked and to be quite honest from a distance it would be very difficult not to mistake her for a woman. Of course this all fell apart at the seams when she became angry and reverted back to her male voice. Those large hands were also a dead giveaway. I would often say to her in my lighter moments. “Do me a cup of tea you saucy cow!” This always went down rather well from those that knew her secret.

My cleaning lady Rosy would be here very soon. We spent more time chatting to each other these days than she did cleaning, we did have a lot in common. A sudden constant overly heavy knock on the door told me that she already knew of my troubles this morning. Then the sound of the key being thrust into the lock. “Morning Jack are you decent?” This was her normal greeting as she opened the door, this was usual and had saved me many a time from confronting her in the raw. “Come on you sod, what have you been up to, now tell Rosy the truth and don’t spare the horses. Brenda down at the café said that you tried to end it all this morning?” I cringed to hear these words as I thought that we had arrived back incognito and had bypassed the obvious. I did show signs of embarrassment at these words winged past me, this was the first time I was beginning to see the serious side of all this. It was time I thought to start lying again as this was my only chance. Would she I thought realise that it was just a load of bullshit, or would she fall for it?

“Rosy my petal, it was just a simple accident and nothing else you must believe me.”
“You lying little shit you tried to end it all and you didn’t confide in me at all and after all the conversations that we have had, shame on you, bloody well shame on you.” At this point I felt like a crock of shit. To think that I could do something

so stupid in the heat of the moment and in turn let all of my friends down. It was like a hot needle going through me. Rosy realised at last that this was not the best way to go with a problem like this. She then sat on the bed next to me and read me the riot act.

"Listen to me you piece of dog shit, we nearly lost you this morning and I couldn't have lived with myself if you had gone and left me without so much as a good bye."
"Well I'm buggered Rosy, I didn't think you cared and here you are throwing yourself at me. Now listen to me you sexy little bint, go and get that other bottle of red from the fridge and we can talk about your desires." We were back on track at last, there was no more telling off, we were adults and the time for reasoning had passed.

The wine flowed for a few hours and things in the apartment gradually settled down, it was then very suddenly that Rosy made her pitch. She sat down on the bed and poured the drinks once again. It was then her time to open up with things and things they were to be sure.

"I've been thinking Jack that you need a woman around here to keep an eye on you and I think I am the one for you. How about we come to an adult agreement?" I must admit that I did straighten myself up in my bed at this comment, but never-the-less I was all ears for her breaking proposal.

"Well Jack we are about the same age, I may possible give you a few years and then maybe not. We are both single and in need of company. So I've been thinking why don't we get it together on a casual no strings attached basis?"
At this juncture I was wondering how was I to react, was it to be my totally shocked and surprised face that I saved up for such occasions, or perhaps it was time to go along for the ride.

"Rosy Brenner I am surprised at you! That must be the best offer I've had in a long time. Get your kit off girl and pronto, then join me for a drink or two. As you know in my present state there won't be any action, I can barely lift my arms up with these chest pains. Get that other bottle of red and then we will be prepared for all eventualities."
Rosy did just that and was soon down to her

underwear and joined me. As she did so there was a certain rummaging around under the bed covers before she found my tackle. We were all set for whatever it was going to be.

She then shuffled around to get herself comfortable before propping herself up alongside me. “Right then Jack, I need to know what drove you to suicide this morning and don’t deny it, your friend Rosy has you sussed. So don’t spare the details, I really want to know so that I can watch out for the tell-tale signs and stop you trying it again.”

“Do you know the name of our new porter Rosy, you will never guess it in a million years and it’s a lot posher than the previous one? He’s called Barnaby.”
“You really are in trouble and have taken a serious beating down in that river. Barnaby has been here for years, you must still be delusional and in shock!” If it wasn’t for Rosy making that comment then I would have thought on in that way, to think that a simple thing like the porter’s name was lost on me made me realise just what I had been through.

Rosy shuffled her way in closer expecting me to open up with some answers. The cramps in my chest and the ringing in my head were starting to stop me thinking once again. Thoughts were now passing through my head of how stupid I was to have even considered this morning actions.
I was starting to feel very sorry for myself having even considered going down that road in the first place, by now I would have been gone for sure and the pleasure of my cleaning ladies new agenda would have missed for ever. It really was better to be alive than a crumpled soggy mess just waiting for the Post Mortem's eventual piece of paper.

"Come on Jack you've had enough time for your own thoughts, now it's time to open up before I squeeze the remaining life out of your nuts."
"Well if you put it that way Rosy, what man could resist your cruel attempts at foreplay. Where by the way did you learn to be so persuasive?"

Rosy did reply, but it was all lost on me for the moment, it was time to try to explain my actions of this morning the best way I could and that wasn't going to be easy let me tell you. We both sat there propped up in bed, both by now slightly pissed, one waiting for an explanation and the other having his nuts in some form of an iron grip. Our glasses were-topped up and it was time to start the story from the top.

“Well it was like this Rosy, it all started the morning I walked into the Riverside café with nothing else on my mind other than the joys of spring.”

The Riverside Café

"Hi Brenda you sexpot, how goes it?"
"None the better for seeing you that's for sure, your usual is it?" I just waited there not really thinking of anything special, passing the time more interested in the passers-by on the footpath below as Brenda sorted out my usual as she called it. "There you go handsome, one large mug of tea, chipped on the edge and spilt down the side just the way you like it and an extra-large bacon sandwich with brown sauce." We'd got off to our normal caustic start, the pleasantries would follow later.

Making my way over to my favourite table in the corner which overlooked the riverside path, it had been kind to me in the past as all manner of misfits and undesirables used the waterside highway. This scant information had helped solve a few of my problems in the past.

A tap on the shoulder had me turning around to the person on the table behind me. It was Doogy Lippers. The advancing years had been very kind

to him and the word on the street was that he was at least eighty five and had seen it all as he once told me. This guy could move around in the community practically un-noticed and was a wealth of local information. We had all known him as kids and many a time he warned us when younger that the police were after us and to make ourselves scarce. “How goes it Doogy?”
“Hi Jack, pretty good for an old un, there’s stuff going on along the footpath, the police have been parked up along there on the look-out for something, what I don’t know. There’s something going down and they’re paying attention!”

I gave him my interested, but amused face as there didn’t seem to be anything else that I could contribute at this stage in the way of conversation. A question or two, soon had things liberated from his overly cautious mind. He did like to be sort of interrogated for the simple answer “Anyone we know Doogy, come on give it to me?”
“Yeah, that new Detective Inspector Trevor Watts, your mate Charlie’s brother, he was waiting parked up with two other officers.”
“Come on Doogy, they wouldn’t let any of those

Watts into the police force as they spent too much time chasing them around the houses down here years ago! ”He just gave me one of his toothless smiles at this comment.
“Nice seeing you Jack, I must be off now, see you about” I reached over to pass him his walking stick and then remembered that it was made from an iron bar. “Still got it then?”
“I wouldn’t go out without it around here.”

Brenda sidled over a few minutes later to get the latest info as she called it. “What’s happening along the riverside path these days, only as I understand it things are becoming a little strange according to Gloria and Dolly? They said that three of the regulars had disappeared in the last few weeks.”
“I expect they have just moved on Brenda like people do, or perhaps the police have been giving them hassle.”
“That’s just it Jack the police never give them bother along the riverside, because as they say they are well out of the way and not causing any trouble.”
“So may I ask why are you telling me all of this?”
“The girls say that you were keeping an eye out for

them from your riverside apartment and they appreciated it."
"That may be true and I only did it from a community point of view, making sure that they were safe as my sister does a bit of business along there at times, just to make ends meet you understand."
"Gloria tells me that she has shown you some extra consideration in the past in-return for your concern towards them."
"That's very true and lovely it was at the time, but that was a few weeks ago and well I don't talk too much about things like that as you well know."
"Jack I have one more thing to tell you and don't get annoyed with me over this, promise?"
"Go on then!"
"I don't know how to say this, but straight out might be the best way. Your sister Sabrina is one of those that's missing."

Well to say it hit me like a ton of bricks would be an understatement. "Are you sure, I was only speaking to her a few days ago?" "I'm sure, that's what the other girls told me!"

I made my way home soon after that little lot settled in and rang my sister. Her flat mate Jane answered and said that she hadn't seen her for about a week and didn't know where she was. Then added the fact that she wasn't in the habit of going anywhere without telling her where and about what time to expect her back.

It was soon after that I rang Charlie and Jim for a get-together. If anyone knew what was happening, they would have the answer. They arrived at the apartment soon after full of questions as to the sudden reason for a summit meeting. "The drinks are in the drinks cabinet boys help yourselves. They were always amused by this as years ago when we were younger it was called the carrier bag in the corner. Help yourself lads and join me on the balcony. It didn't take too much to encourage these two to pour themselves a little something and before I knew it they were baying at the bit for the update.

"Come on Jack we don't get the call that often these days what's this all about then?" "Sabi has gone missing, I just wondered if you had heard anything as I am getting worried, it's been at least a week according to Jane and so far not a word. It's not like Sabi to do anything like this and well, I just thought maybe you two had some insight into this." They clearly hadn't a clue, we consumed a few more drinks and then harked back to our school days and the fun we had as kids.

Charlie was the one for the memory lane stuff. "Do you remember our trips up the gas tank on those special tours you reserved for the tourists as you called us and those paper aeroplanes we used to fly off the top? You and your brother were completely mad and I will never forget the daft things we used to get up to following you and Peter."
"They were special days to be sure boys and it was a pleasure to amuse you and take a few bob off you lot to boost our coffers so to speak!
Well, if you do hear anything about Sabi, then let me know a bit quick as I'm getting very concerned as to her safety."

We all sat there crammed onto my balcony slowly getting pissed. Charlie as usual had his feet spread eagled on top of the balcony rail, while Jim although slightly more astute practised his quick get-away for the drinks top up. This wasn't the first time and probably not the last that this lot would come around and raid my drinks cabinet. I mean carrier bag.

Sabrina

"When's the rent due Jane only I'm a bit skint this month, perhaps it's time to go and earn some proper wages down on the walk. I will only go for a few hours, you never know I could get lucky with a nice punter." Sabi left soon after, the walk along the riverside was always a pleasure taking in the early evening air, accompanied by those twinkling lights that were dotted along the pathway and the gentle rippling of that downstream current. I soon came across Gloria and we stood there chatting until she picked up a customer and was soon off earning.

Dolly appeared out of the shadows and we spent a further few minutes passing the time of day before she also got some business. I was by now alone waiting for some action that maybe that night wouldn't materialise.

The next thing I heard was the sound of Doogy's walking stick with its single tap-tap as he struggled along the riverside path. Doogy always wore those carpet slippers and would sometimes creep up on

you, he was slowly getting closer by the minute. I spoke to him well before he reached me as the last time I made him jump out of his skin. "Hi Doogy, been up that pub again have we?"
"Hello Sabi, still at it are you, on the game?"
"Are you looking for some business, I haven't had an old bugger like you for ages. I tell you what, I'll give that walking stick of yours a massage for a fiver, how's that?"
"Bugger off you brazen cow, I wouldn't let you get anywhere near it. Oh by the way the police are parked up along the stony road that leads down from the pub." "Thanks Doogy, but they won't bother me, see you."

Off he went plodding along muttering to himself until I could hear him no more. I was just about to give up when a rather smart looking man approached me. "Are you looking for business?" he said well before he reached me. "What have you got in mind, I replied rather quickly?"

"I have a place further up the river, how about we spend a few hours there. Everything seemed okay so we walked in the general direction that he indicated. I then text Jane and told her I wouldn’t be back until later and not to worry

Brenda

"Come on you lot, haven't you got homes to go to, I need to get this cafe cleaned up and finished for the day, or do you want me to get into trouble with my wife!"

Some of the stragglers would hang on to the bitter end forcing me to become sterner with them than was my usual way. "Shift it will ya." It wasn't long after that the place was in darkness as I locked it up again for the night. Bye bye to the smell of bacon fat and sweaty bodies for another night I thought to myself as I descended the steps on the bridge for the umpteenth time this week.

My usual walk home along the riverside often brought me in contact with my friends that were out on the strip as they called it plying their wares for the early evening trade. I was anxious to get home as I bumped into the first of them that night "Hi Dolly, you still at it trying for an early one." "Hiya Brenda, have you seen Jack today only things are getting desperate? Sabi still hasn't made contact, Gloria and I reckon it's time to call

the police and get them involved."
"Yeah, saw him this morning and broke it to him in my usual way, like straight down the line. On my way home I will call in and see Jane just to make sure she's okay and then there is nothing else we can do as I see it!"
"How's your boy doing Brenda, I haven't seen him for ages, he must be growing up fast and going to school by now?"
"Yes, Darren's nearly seven, he likes school, but often comes home with problems to solve like homework, the other day he came home in tears as some kid or other reckoned one of his mums was called Nelly poof. I couldn't at his age explain anything to him, but that's kids for you I suppose. I told him if he says it again to tell him you have two mums and he has only one, see you later."
"One more thing Brenda, is Annabelle pregnant, only I saw her in the bakers and she was showing signs."
"No no, nothing like that, it's the cream cakes, see ya?" I did manage at last to get home after a short chat with Gloria who I bumped into further along the footpath.

"Hi Anna, how's it been today?"
"No problems, but Darren needs you, he's in the other room with a problem that he thinks only you can solve!" We both looked each other before I turned to confront it all once again.

"Hello Darren, had a good day at school have you?" Darren hesitated for a second. "Yes okay mum, can you fix my aeroplane for me?"
"Where did you get that from?"
"Found it floating in the river, one of the other boys got one as well."
I just looked at the soggy mess. "It's become unfolded and water logged, it's too complicated for me, but I know someone who used to make these when he was a kid. We can dry it out overnight by the fire and I will take it with me tomorrow and if he comes in I will get him to refold it for you, how's that?" Darren gave me one of his satisfied smiles, looks like we solved that little problem I thought as we settled down for the evening's television.

Police station

I had spent the early morning sat on my balcony contemplating on whether to visit the police station or not, for me it wasn't the most welcoming place in this world.

I did what the desk Sargent told me to do after he asked about the nature of my enquiry. He needed some information as to the reason for my visit before asking me to sit down. I waited there anxiously for some sort of attention. There were all sorts of comings and goings in a place like this and although this wasn't my first time, the things we did in the past where more or less of a minor nature and none of it was as serious as this.

When we were kids we would often be escorted into this place by our ears, as a burly police officer who had had enough of our silly nonsense responded in kind. To say it was all minor stuff would be correct, but never-the-less it took up valuable police time and wasn't to be tolerated. The desk Sargent called me over after half an hour or so had passed and explained that they were short of officers to deal with my enquiry. I could either come back another day, or hang on for some time and if they had someone available then they would deal with me, but no promises.

My patience paid off as at last I was escorted into a back office and introduced to the man himself DI Trevor Watts of all people. I didn't mention my friendship with his notorious brother Charlie, but there again I didn't need to, he just looked at me and remembered who I was from our little meetings from my earlier life. "Ah, Mr Jack Sparrow we meet again in rather different circumstances than all of the times before. So after all of the problems you gave us when you were younger, you now come in here looking for help! Well I'll be blowed. I feel like just throwing you out on the street and letting you sort this thing out yourself. " This was their way with things to put you on the back foot, to them it was always a good starting point. I really did need their help with this matter and started off by calling him Sir.

This was soon nipped in the bud as he told me to get on with it and tell him what my problem was. "My sister Sabrina Sparrow has gone missing and her flat mate Jane says it's unlike her to just go off and not tell her where and what time she would be back. It's been at least a week and none of us have heard anything at all."

"You will have to fill in a missing persons form and leave it with us. We wouldn't even consider doing anything about it for a few more weeks as lots of people go off and then return a few days or weeks later, it happens all of the time.
I suggest you complete the form and if she hasn't returned in about another week or so then come back with a recent photograph and we will take it from there."
I wasn't satisfied with this brush off. "You don't seem to understand officer there are at least two other people that have disappeared in the last week or so, it's not only my sister."

He then gave me a shock answer. "If that's the case Mr Sparrow why haven't others complained of the same thing?" He had a point, was I the only one to have reported it, I suppose I was.
I left the police station shortly afterwards none the wiser scratching my head. It was so easy to say, but it didn't make any sense at all. Why were

we all panicking over nothing, or was there something else to all of this.

The detective's words were to haunt me in the next few hours as I waited for the night-shift to start down on the riverside walk. Darkness at this time of year would come early, so the anxiety of the wait would be short lived. Indeed darkness was soon upon me and I made my way slowly at first looking for the people of the night.

I came across Gloria first who had just made a contact and was walking off with her trick to complete the deal. So I just nodded as she passed. Dolly was nowhere to be found. There was only one thing for it and that was to wait patiently for one of them to return.

I sat back on a slatted bench and tucked myself into the shadows. The detective's words echoed through my mind more than once as I sat there patiently observing the twinkling lights bouncing across the water. It was then that the far off noise of Doogy's walking stick attracted my attention. We all knew the sound as he proceeded along and more than once us kids would jump out of the bushes and scare the shit out of him, but this night

I was on a mission to observe the goings on and my so called days of fun had passed me by in my adult life.

Doogy passed by oblivious as to my presence. The next people to pass were a courting couple snogging there way along the riverside, every three or four paces they would have to stop to get back at it again. A smart looking man then strolled past and looked around as he walked along. I had seen that walk before and it reminded me of someone, who, for the life of me I couldn't remember where. A short time later the clicking of Dolly's extra high stiletto heels attracted my attention tapping along the tarmac path. I was just about to reveal myself so as not to surprise her when the sound of a man's voice pulled me back into the shadows. They passed a short time later arm in arm and then were gone into the darkness of the night.

So my first stake out of the riverside-walk had completely been a waste of time, the evening had moved on apace and there was nothing else for it, but to creep my way back home. I was Just about to jump to my feet as the sound of Doogy's stick sounded out once again echoing along the river. I must admit at the time it did go through my mind to jump out and put the shits up him, but well maybe I had really grown up at last and he was these days a good passing friend as you might say. So I did the decent thing.

"Hi Doogy, it's Jack, you haven't been up that pub again getting pissed have you?"
"Why do you Sparrows always give me stick as I pass, Sabi did it to me last time and now you, can't a bloke have a quiet drink with some company these days without the two of you chiding me, now sod-off." That was my cue to bid him goodnight and get myself home. He will be all fun tomorrow when he sobers up and he will see it as just a bit of fun.

The next morning

I'd had a restless night worrying about my sister. I just couldn't get it out of my head that I was the only one that had reported her missing. Jane had asked me to do it, but she didn't even consider doing it herself and waited for me to take the initiative.

I had always had my suspicions about Jane as there were other times that their friendship as flat mates didn't quit seem to gel. It was as if she wanted the place to herself. So then I asked myself why she didn't ring me when Sabi didn't return that evening, she waited for me to ring her a week later. It was all starting to become something else in my mind and not at all as it seemed on the surface.

I was of a gullible nature and would take things said at face value, not ever dreaming that people were as good at telling lies as I was at believing them.

I had inadvertently started to take this thing on myself. A short visit last night just to ask Gloria, or whoever else was available for some information, had seen me ending up on a stakeout. To me it appeared to be the right way to do things, but sleuthing was all very new to me and maybe I had missed the obvious.

It was time once again for my usual from the Riverside Café. The thing here was to get past Barnaby the porter without being seen, as failure to do so could have him bending your ear for half an hour. My luck was in, he wasn't at his little sliding security window. I managed to duck below it and thought to myself nice one, only to be confronted by some other person who was a complete stranger to me. "Hello resident, trying to sneak out were we?"
"Who are you, only this is supposed to be Barnaby's patch, or so I thought?"
"Yes it is, I'm Simon by the way the new man on the block, in the last few weeks we've had a rota change, Barnaby is now working the week-ends as well. So he gets a couple of days off, you will have to put up with me on Thursdays and Fridays from now on."

"Looks like I'm safe Simon for at least two days of the week then!"
"Yes he does go on a bit, that's because he's still recovering from some form of stress after his mother died, which has left him without anyone to talk to."
"Ah right, I see."

I pondered my way along the footpath looking mainly at the ground as was my way when trying to sort things out in my head. Brenda got in there first this morning as I entered. "Morning sex-pot, how would you like it?" I wasn't in the mood for the silly nonsense, it was too early for all of that so I just made signs with my hands to indicate a bacon sandwich and a mug of tea, then moved slowly to my table in the corner, trying to think this thing through.

I apologised to Brenda when she eventually brought my usual over. "Sorry about that rather poor entrance, but I have things on my mind." Brenda just accepted that people did suffer from moods at times and this was one of mine. She didn't say anything as she placed my bacon sandwich in front of me and the mug of tea. A third item then caught my eye as she lowered another plate down on the table with what looked like a paper aeroplane on it that had seen some severe action. “Darren and his mate found two paper aeroplanes in the river and he wants you to refold it for him. I said you were the man.”

I didn’t answer, but just picked it up. It was rather well made and exactly the same method that I used as a kid. It was made form a sheet of school book exercise paper complete with pencilled air craft number JS-112B, there was some other writing that had all but disappeared due to its extended soaking. This did take me back along way and cleared any previous smouldering thoughts from my mind.

This little plane really needed to be un-folded and re-folded back up the other way to give it the necessary sharp edges, which I quickly set about. The pencilled writing now forming a camouflaged patchwork. I then creased a few edges before attracting Brenda from across the dining room. “Here we go girl, see what you think of this?” The plane flew past a few of the customer’s noses before being caught by a bemused Brenda, she mouthed back. “Thank you Jack, Darren will be pleased!”

Charlie and Jim were the next to come in and settled down at the table. Charlie was the first to speak as usual. “Any Luck with your enquiries about Sabi?”
“I’ll tell you something Charlie, I was of all places down at the police station yesterday talking to your brother about all of this and he wasn’t too interested in what I had to say.”
“That’s your reputation going before you Jack, that is!” “Coming from you Charlie that’s a joke. Perhaps Trevor doesn’t know that it was you that climbed up the town hall clock tower and took the hands off the clock.”
“I didn’t think you would remember that Jack.”
“Just one of those things I keep on the back burner as a little insurance against spurious false stories and slander.”

Jim just sat there listening to all of this, he was more of a thinker than Charlie. Charlie would just dive in, but Jim was always right when he did get around to speaking. “Have you been down and talked to the girls on the riverside yet Jack?”

"Yes, I went last night and in the end I started to stake the place out, but not really knowing where the beginning of all of this was, I found it difficult to put anything together."
Jim was throwing himself into it as he said the very thing that all of this needed. "You need to find the last person to see her and then work backwards towards a solution. Which in turn with give you the ending."

Charlie and I just sat there not really understanding all of it, but the logic of it was obvious even to us, Jim was the way to go and my amateurish efforts were without substance. Jim started up again.
"All you need to do is find the people that go along there all the time and ask them some questions, they must have seen something, it's one of those things and most people forget to remember, because they don't need to."

It had all suddenly sprung to life, there was a certain logic to all of this and Jim had given me the heads-up.
"Right boys a list of witnesses to be drawn up right now. We three go along there often." Charlie

protested. “We don’t count now do we?”
“Oh yes we do,” said Jim. “Everyone that goes along there is a potential witness, all of us included.”
“We need the three names of those girls that have disappeared first, so we know who we’re talking about.” I was at last starting to get the drift on all of this, prompted on by Jim. So let’s make a list first. Sabi was one, perhaps Brenda knows the other names?”

I walked over to Brenda who was by now my best mate after the aeroplane fix. She soon furnished me with the details.

The others could tell from my cocky smile as I returned that that things were working out. “Here we go, got the names, but only their first names as Brenda only knows them from chatting to them on the way home.

“So here we go, Sheila was the first to disappear, then Caroline followed by Sabi. The first one was three weeks ago and the second was a fortnight ago and Sabi was last week. They all looked at each other with the same words on their lips. “That’s exactly one person a week. Already things are starting to add up," said Jim. "Now all we need is a list of names of the people that use the riverside path on a regular basis and then we can start to ask some questions."

Charlie at last was getting into all of this. "Brenda walks along there twice every day, along with us three, Doogy is always along there creeping about in the dark. Why do they call him Doogy Lippers by the way, I've always wondered? "

"It's on account of him always wearing slippers because of his bad feet and he can't pronounce Dougal slippers properly and never could. It all started when he was at school." "Ah right, so that's it."

I sat there quietly thinking out loud, so one has gone every week for the last three weeks. There wasn't one this week, why's that I wonder? I was trying my best to be logical about things and not get emotionally involved because of my sister which would cloud my thinking. There was a clue here somewhere, but where, it looked to me as more time would have to pass before things started to gel together.

“How about we go back to my place lads and have a drink or two?” They were well up for it and the company would help me to get over my present predicament.

Jim did the drinks as usual from my drinks cabinet, Charlie had already made himself comfortable with his feet up on the balcony rail. We spent a happy afternoon drinking the day away. Jim was insistent and asked his burning question. “How about one of your stories Jack, we used to love them when we were kids. Can you still tell them? How about that one about the computer guy and his wife”
“I can’t believe you still remembered it, it was all about being patient with people. It was called the keyboard warrior, here we go.

The keyboard warrior

Dave and Margo were a devoted couple until it came to that computer in the corner.

“Show me how to do this on the computer Dave, I just keep making a mess of it.”
”Well, that’s not too difficult, why do you struggle with such simple things? You just do this, then hit

that button there."
"Slow down, it's no good you just rattling through it, I need to see how it's done, not how fast you can do it. Now do it again slowly so I can take a few crib notes down as you go along."

Dave was a whiz on the keyboard, there wasn't much he couldn't do. Margo as he called her on the other hand would struggle with the wretched thing until she had familiarised herself with each stoke of the keys on any particular problem, after that she was well away, problem sorted as she would say the next time.

Margo had the patience, Dave was a blusterer. You may go as far as calling him a cocky sod, never understanding why Margo would struggle on such a simple task.

"Go through that part again!" She demanded. Dave would overly slow down to the point of piss taking to make his point. "When you've done that, then slide your fingers along the key board until you get to the enter key, this one here, that's if you can find it, shall I cover it with tape and write on it the word PUSH."

There was soon going to be a bust up, Margo was starting to blow a fuse, but kept things just about under control until she finally understood. "I just needed to download a recipe, you know the one for your favourite cake. There is a new recipe out that was in my magazine, but we can forget that now as I don't reckon you're worth a cake." "Now, now, my little honey pot, don't take on so, listen my little buttercup you know I was only joking, don't you?" "Yeah right mate of course I did, that won't alter the fact that you are not getting it and how's that for a happy ending. The only thing that you understand well is sarcasm."

There was a sombre tone in the home as these two avoided passing each other for the next few hours. When the time of silence had passed, Dave made his first verbal contact. "Are you still upset at my crass remarks?"
"No not really, but the only way you will get that cake is if you make it yourself Buddy boy." He thought on for a while and chewed over those sinister sounding words, maybe I could do it for myself, it can't be that hard as Margo can do a cake without thinking, just a bit of that then stir in

some of this and Hey Presto the beauty arrives all hot and steamy.

The scene was set, he would show her a thing or two. “Okay, I will make the cake myself, on my own with no help from you the next time you go out and leave me in peace.!”
“You what! You couldn’t bake a cake, remember you’re the one that put the Shepherd’s pie in the oven with the cling film still on it, remember?”
“I only did what the note said and that was to take it out of the fridge and put it in the oven on gas mark 5 at 11 o’clock, it never said to remove the cling film, so I didn’t.”
“Common sense would have told you to do that, your skill ends at that keyboard, the rest of it you don’t even know.”

“You must admit it was the crustiest pie we’ve ever had though wasn’t it?” “Margo nearly cracked at this comment, just about holding back a smile. “If you think that you can do it then have a go, we will see how you manage without that recipe and me guiding you through.”
“I have seen you do it before and always wondered why you would need a recipe in the

first place, a recipe is just a set of jump leads connected to an experienced baker, that's all"

"So when are we in for this little treat?"
"I will complete the task next time you go out with Veronica and have the thing of beauty waiting for you on your return, how's that. Would you like to place a bet on it, or just a handshake?"
"I don't want to touch your grubby little hand, the bets on, you will never do it." Things were still simmering between them as Dave replied.
"We will see about that my little buttercup!"

This was the point of no return and he knew it, the words had been uttered, the bet was on, the keyboard warrior had spoken.

There was a dusty silence in the household for the next few days as his stealth plans were laid. Writing down the moves he had seen her do when baking that cake before, the order of these were checked and computed. He was on to it like a ton of bricks. A nonchalant swagger followed him around as his cocky arrogance by now knew no bounds.

"Hi Veronica, all set to go are we, there will be a treat waiting for us when we get back, him in there is going to bake us a lovely cake for tea."
"I'm jealous, my Bob couldn't even get near to that."

"Bye you two, have a nice day, just one thing Rosebud, the cooker how does it switch on and which knob is it?"
"Oh that's really easy, you just do this, then this and then push that, if you can't find it just run your fingers along the knobs until you get to this one and then push, it's easy. I could stick some tape on it with the word PUSH if it would make things easier."
"Let me just write that down!"
"Why do you need crib notes, you're kidding me, it's all so easy, you should be able to remember that, Bye"

Veronica looked at Margo thinking she had been a little hard on Dave for no real reason. With that he was soon on his own.

What do we need to start with, oh yes that blender thing. Then we need flour, that sort there should do it, half a bag that looks about right. Now for some butter, what do you reckon about half a slab in on top, yes that's about right? Don't forget the sugar, well done. Two pours of that stuff. How many eggs shall we give it? Well there are six in the box, must be all of them, so far so good. Currants or sultanas, I'm not sure, easy answer half and half. What was that white powder stuff that you need half a teaspoon of? It isn't salt, that's over there and was something in a cardboard tub. Rummaging through the spice draw he came across the very thing, in went half a spoonful. Now time to give it a swirl. Oops forgot the milk.

Leaving it to blend properly is part of the secret that I do know. Within no time at all the mix was looking the dogs, perhaps the sultanas had suffered a bit in that machine, but otherwise we were ready to go.

Cake tin, some of that brown paper stuff inside, I'm no slouch. Tippy in nicely, there she was, the thing of beauty ready for the off. Pouring himself a glass of wine and readying himself for the long cooking cycle it was time to sort out that cooker.

That knob there, yes that looks fine and then this, then push that one, the whole thing started up a treat. Warm up the oven first, we don't start with a cold oven now do we. Bottom shelf for a slow cooking time, yes that bits okay. Cover the top over with the remains of the brown paper to stop it burning and away we go. Sitting back Dave was in his element, sorted first time he consoled himself with a further couple of glasses of the red stuff. Just for his effort.

Right next job tidy things up and clear down the work surfaces, we don't want things to look as if there has been any panic. A few hours passed and the smell emanating all around the house told him of his success.

Dave just sat there with a stupid looking grin on his face as the two shoppers eventually returned. The two ladies looked at each other, judging by the aroma there was success in the air. There must have been a few negative comments between them while they were out that he wasn't privy to.

"So there we have it my master piece, I will make a cup of tea. You two ladies just relax while I

get things ready. The table now laid the threesome sat down for the treat. The top of the cake had sunk a little, being passed off as, that is how I like things and it was duly sliced up. At this point there were gasps of admiration from the spectators until they looked at the thing of beauty. The centre was sloppy and uncooked.
They refused to eat it, Dave dived in consuming two rather large slices before placing it back into the cake tin. A few days later a rather sinister looking mould started to appear, undeterred the key board warrior treated himself again.

The E.coli infection was accompanied by several visits to the doctors, Margo was responsible for administering the tablets as Dave by now was very weak. "How do you get the lid off of this container Margo?"
“You just do this, then that and then push that there, I can put some tape on the lid with the word PUSH written on it if you like Dave!

The boys had just sat back sipping their drinks, totally entertained. "Bloody cracker that Jack, I’ve always admired you for those stories, how do you do it?"

"Well that's for me to know and for you two to be jealous of."

Into the dark

The day had gone very well and a few more parts to the puzzle were starting to come together. The boys left me a short time later much the worse for wear, as they staggered off to their respective homes. With dusk settling in it was nearly time to re-visit the riverside walk and maybe this time get some information from those girls?

I made myself walk slowly along the footpath as the twinkling lights flickered across the water. In my eagerness to make contact with just about anyone I had departed too early. As I suspected there was no one there this early in the evening, so I decided to walk on down as far as the bridge which would take half an hour or so.

An occasional splash in the water indicated that the trout were starting to feed again after the long cold winter. Another much larger splash followed soon after the first and then by another had me thinking a different reason. As I approached the bridge it was at last obvious as to what was causing it. I pressed myself into the shadows of the shrubbery trying to ascertain where the splashing was coming from. At last pinpointing it to be coming from someone up on the railway bridge.

If there ever was a time for silence and observation then this was surely it. What would someone want with dropping packages off of a railway bridge after dark? There was only one reason that came to my mind and that was disposing of something in mid-stream. What was the reason for that do you suppose? I questioned myself a few more times before the culprit showed himself.

Well at last the person had revealed themselves, I moved slowly forwards to extricate myself from the surrounding foliage, but to no avail, the darkness and the bushes had foiled any identification, but why was I at all interested I asked myself. All I knew was that they rode a bike and an old one at that judging by the clanking sound it made as he pedalled along and that was it. I waited until the coast was clear and made my way quickly to where the splashing had come from.

The forceful current had by now flung them far out into midstream and way out of reach. I had no real reason to retrieve them anyway. If someone wants to get rid of a few dead cats, or whatever it's up to them I suppose. For that was the usual reason for things being thrown into the river? It did at the time seem a little too contrived to go to so much trouble for what could have only been rubbish.

Well it had consumed some time I suppose and that was the main purpose for my extended walk in the first place. Walking back along the river I reached the gasometers. This was Dolly's patch and all of her clients knew where to find her. There was no Dolly today, she had probably landed a client and was busy making her money. It was time for a trip up to where Gloria hung out and my last chance this night of getting some information.

Arriving at Gloria's patch left me in no doubt that she had been attacked in some way. There were what looked like the contents of a handbag spilled out and laying all over the footpath. The whole place was splattered with blood. Something dreadful had occurred and while I was in the area. None of this was there when I passed by earlier. I just stood there wondering what had happened when in the distance I heard the sound of that clanking bicycle approaching fast.

The very one from earlier that evening down at the bridge. I once again tucked myself back into the shadows as it passed by. I was none the wiser for my efforts, having gleaned no more information than before, a bike with a male rider breathing heavily clanking its way past. There was just one last hope and that was to position myself in a place of good light and take a casual stroll towards him on his return trip, which in my judgement would be in about half an hour.

I decided there and then that the only place to be was at the junction of that side road at the back of the Riverside Café where it joined the riverside path. It was back up along the pathway about ten minutes away. There was a lamp-post there and it was my only chance. I quickly arrived and got myself into position to await the cyclist, who I hoped at last I could identify. My plan was to be back past the lamp-post in the shadows and slowly walk forward into the light as I heard him clanking his approach, intercepting him as we both approached the lamplight together. I was all set.

A further ten minutes or so passed until I could hear him making his way back. I need to get the timing just right and slowly stepped out of the shadows into the light as he approached. Suddenly a heavy hand clamped over my mouth pulling me back into the shadows and throwing me down to the ground. “It’s me, Charlie, keep out of this, it’s not your business Jack!” The cyclist passed on by without any hesitation. “Come on then Charlie, we have been together all day drinking and suddenly you are not on my side anymore, what gives mate and I want it straight.”

“Take it from me Jack its best you keep out of all of this, Jim and I have it covered and that’s all you have to know for the time being. Don’t mention this to anyone, don’t talk to the porter whatever you do and keep shtum, or you will blow this lot out of the water. We knew you would be on the look-out tonight from what you said this afternoon. You could end up in serious trouble over this and then we would have to keep an eye out for you as well. Now listen to me, be a good boy Jack and forget it for this evening whatever you do, there is stuff going down here and you're not part of it.

Now go home, I will try and explain things tomorrow, but remember don't talk to anyone, or that will be the end of you for sure." I did challenge him for more information, but when Charlie was insistent, you didn't argue too much.

I made my way back to the apartment wondering what the hell I had got myself mixed up in. My old mum always said to me when things get messy, or you don't understand what's going on, come home quick and don't get involved in it. It was one of those occasions and I knew it was time to get out fast.

The porter tried to ask me questions as I passed. "I have a package for you Jack, you will have to sign for it." I had heard Charlie's advice and heeded it .Making my way up to my apartment the shaking was starting to take me over. At last the safety of my flat was the most welcoming sight of all.

I sat there curtains drawn in the darkness, the only consoling thing was a glass of red and a few puffs on my e-ciggy. I had been taken over with fear in just a few minutes of this little lot kicking off.

Charlie had said not to say anything, but he didn't tell me not to think. The curiosity was by now uppermost in my mind as I crawled on hands and knees toward my balcony door. With the light still off I slowly eased the curtains back and the doors open, then slid myself along on my belly towards the balcony rail. Re-arranging the flower pots gave me a camouflaged view of the riverside path. I adopted my patient but inquisitive mode. This wasn't going to be a quick fix by any stretch of the imagination, patience would be of the essence.

From my perch I could see the side-road by the Riverside Café and those bushes where I knew Charlie was hiding. I hadn't been watching for very long before the cyclist re-appeared with a large rucksack on his back. He was pedalling like fury, the clanking sound emanating along the path as he progressed along noisily toward the railway bridge once again. At first I didn't notice the police car with its extinguished lights arriving and silently creeping forward toward the end of side-road and coming to a rest in the shadows just short of where the road intersected the footpath. There was going to be a connection of some sort when that cyclist re-appeared, I could feel it.

It was a short while after that I heard the clanking sound of the cyclist returning. Whether Charlie had nodded off, or he was playing a blinder with the police, I could only imagine. Doogy was the next to appear as he made his way slowly past the police car and on into the bushes. A second or so had lapsed before he continued on his way. Doogy must have twigged onto their presence as he passed and done the decent thing as they say. Suddenly the bushes parted and a very casual Charlie trolled almost nonchalantly along the footpath passing within inches of the front of the police car as if it wasn't there, he had made his move.

He suddenly broke into a sprint, waving his arms at the cyclist and flashing a light. The next thing to happen quite amused me and it was the sound of two large splashes filling the air. That'll be the bicycle and the rucksack going for a swim I thought. I retreated backwards into my apartment for another drink still pondering about the activity that was going on down on the footpath.

The thought of not knowing who that cyclist was had me momentarily heading back to the balcony, I just had to know for sure. Two shadowy figures emerged and then disappeared between each lamppost as they passed from the light then back into the shadows between the lights. Eventually they reached the point just below my balcony and the connection was made. Charlie and Jim Sheen moved with a startled look about them as two burly police officers unknown to them approached from the direction of the police car. I wanted to shout a warning, but that's not much fun now is it, I thought as the inevitable was just about to happen, let them get on with it was the only conclusion to draw.

From my vantage point I could see what would happen next and it did. The four of them nearly bumped into each other in the darkness. I expected a couple of arrests to follow, but oh no, they were laughing between themselves. Charlie repeated something gesticulating with his hands that set them off again. Before they parted company there were handshakes all round accompanied by smiles and back slapping. You just couldn't make it up. I crawled back into my apartment for the second time unnoticed. I had to pour myself another drink to even try to get my head around all of this.

Let's have a look at things that had occurred this evening and only because I decided as suggested by Jim that I needed to have a word with the girls down along the footpath. Firstly there wasn't any of them there. Secondly someone was throwing stuff into the river off the railway bridge. Thirdly Charlie catches me and warns me off the sleuthing and then they nearly get caught doing something and all end up shaking hands and laughing together with the police. I just scratched my head, it was all well beyond me that was for sure.

It had been a traumatic night as I settled down in the hope of sleep, it all meant something, but what? Well perhaps the morning would bring some answers.

The crack of dawn

Sleep failed to visit me last night and I was up and about well before the sun had settled on my balcony with its brittle early morning rays. I seemed to be doing a lot of this early morning stuff just lately, not at all like years ago when I had to be prised from my bed in the mornings.

I did eventually make the balcony for the early morning sun and rested up for a while trying not to think about yesterday. I had a package to collect from the porter later on today, that can wait until I wake up a bit. I was still there a few hours later when those two little kids that were always fishing along the riverbank just below me, appeared with what looked like a grappling hook tied to a piece of rope. Something we all did as kids and a variation of things were pulled out. One day we landed a gun that had probably been tossed into the river from a passing train, or so we thought at the time.

They weren't trying their luck at different places as we did when we were kids, but seemed to heading for a particular spot. The hook and rope were thrown out as far as their little arms could manage each time pulling it back in to retrieve any booty. It wasn’t long before the bike was hooked and joyously inspected by the two of them. A couple of more tries had the ruck sack sorted out and on the bank being greedily inspected for any treasure. They did manage to get something from one of the side pockets and quickly shared it out between them stuffing it in their pockets. From where I was I couldn’t tell just what it was, but to them it was like gold dust.

I knew there was something organised about this little excursion and I was proven to be right when Charlie appeared further along the footpath and slipped them something for their troubles. He then rode off on the bike with the dripping wet rucksack slung over his shoulder and disappeared. My balcony garden had kept me well concealed while this little exercise was being completed.

The burglary

Well to say that last night was a nerve racking experience would be an understatement as I shakily poured my first cup of coffee of the day, my mind was just about in control of the remains of my body. Our normal meeting place was the Riverside Café. So I decided to venture out and show myself once again, nothing could be as bad as the previous evening, or so I thought as I made my way down through the entrance hall. Barnaby must have a sixth sense to have caught me as I tip toed past his office.

"Hi Jack, nice to see you this morning all bright and fresh after last night's antics!" I wasn't being drawn into a conversation with the likes of him. "I have a package for you, hang on."
"I'm just going out for a while, I will pick it up when I return." I quickly left the building before he had a chance to reply.

Brenda was well on form as I opened the door and caught me off guard with her usual randy approach. "Hi Sexy boy, in need this morning are

you?"
"Yes petal, very much in need and you have the very thing I know will put me right in this world." She was well aware not to cross swords with me as she would always end up on the losing side and she knew it, but that didn't stop her trying it on most mornings. She looked expectantly at me waiting for a response. "My usual please." I spotted Doogy the very man who had last night tipped off Charlie as he hid up in the bushes.

"Hi Doogy, what gives after last night's action?" He just looked at me with that innocent face he saved up for such occasions. "What me Jack, you know me, straight as a die and you know it?" I could see that's about as far as that one was going. "Do you want to buy a phone Jack? I found this one just down there in the bushes a few days ago." It was a nice phone and it was found in the same spot that Charlie was hiding in last night, so I asked him how much he wanted for it. "A bacon sandwich and a cup of tea, no questions." I asked Brenda to double my usual and slipped the phone into my pocket.

Charlie and Jim were the next to come in and they beckoned me over to the corner table. This was what I had waited for and I wasn't about to instigate the conversation first. Charlie opened up in his usual brusque way. "You okay Jack with this world?"
"Just about boys, but only just."
"I suppose you want to know what was going on last night do you?"
"It might be an idea to let me in on things so as I don't tread on your toes anymore." Jim chipped in. "We were only being cautious because we have a little business thing going on and you were getting in the way of things."
"Wasn't it you Jim that said the next thing to do was to ask the girls down on the footpath a few questions? I was only doing what you suggested and nothing else. I am not in the slightest bit interested in what you get up to, I just want to find my sister and that's all, got it?"

Charlie then looked at me. "Let's forget it Jack, it didn't happen."
"Sod off you two, I'm not going to forget it just like that, why should I?" I couldn't have cared less what they we up to and I didn't want to know. The

less I knew, the less I was involved and that's the way I wanted it, but whatever it was, it was serious enough to cause them panic when that police car arrived. It was time for a common sense rethink and it was now down to me to lead myself out of this mess that I had just talked myself into. "You're right lads, it didn't happen, I was over reacting there, it won't happen again. We ended up all smiles.

Charlie then enquired about Sabi. "Any luck with the girls down on the footpath last night?" That was I thought a strange question as they were both along there themselves and knew there was no one there all evening. To keep things on a level playing field, I just replied. "No change." It was time to go and get myself some quality time back at the apartment. "I'm heading off home now lads, the day is going too fast for me!"

They insisted I stayed a bit longer and then started to ask me questions about the disappearance of those girls. Charlie wanted to know if I knew which day of the week it was that they disappeared and did I know that Gloria had been mugged? I had an idea that Gloria had been in some sort trouble, but which day of the week those girls disappeared had caught me out, as I had no idea. It was only when I mentioned that it was about time to revisit the police station that they really re-acted.

Jim was straight in there and tried to persuade me to leave it a bit longer and not to annoy the police unnecessarily. The whole bloody thing didn't add up. Here was these two up to everything last night and running away from the police and now they were trying to talk me out of talking to them again, it just didn't make any sense.

They were employing time wasting tactics for some reason and they were trying to steer me away from contacting the police, but I didn't know why, so I played along. "How about another one of your stories Jack and then we will let you go for a while?" It was time to lay one on them. "I have just the one for a couple of crooks like you."

The apprentice burglar

The cold dark prison cell was starting to have an effect on the new inmate, lights out at 11 o'clock with no concessions, whatever the excuse. Sleeping three to a cell was just about the worst thing ever. Snoring, grunts and the occasional talking did nothing for Mel's beauty sleep. The other two were a right miss mash of the human species to be sure.

Bob had the IQ of a dead sheep, while Tony although a lot brighter spent the whole day telling us of how he managed to lift a couple of hundred quid from the bookies and of his other exploits, all this he said made him rich. That's not what we saw, we saw a blown out old guy on his last legs, bragging constantly of how he had been so successful up until the time he was caught.

The daily slopping out in the mornings was on a rota basis. Everything was done by the clock, breakfast, lunch and evening meal was timed to the second with no variations. Being cooped up in that cell for 24 hours a day with those two and that stinking slop bucket was the worst thing ever. And all for what?

It can't be that difficult thought Mel. What do we need to do? First select a property that has a well-hidden garden preferable with high hedges, no children's toys about, along with a complete absence of dogs. Right then let's have a little look around the neighbourhood. Mel had hit the hard times unemployed for almost a year, the austerity measures had effected the very meagre income that he was receiving, namely the dole money. Things were on a downward path and had been going that way for ages. It really was time to drop the cheap fiddles of working on the side for peanuts. The big-time was beckoning, he would do it.

The neighbourhood was scoured and the net result was a small house tucked away behind some trees. This one seemed to fit the bill! Right my son, we will case that joint in daylight tomorrow. These being the words they used on the telly to describe such operations, then that must be the right way to do things. Mel chewed his collar for the umpteenth time that evening wondering just how much booty this little operation was going to release.

The very next day Mel cased the joint, as he was observing a little old lady left the house with her shopping bags. She looks just like my Granny he thought to himself, what a lovely old lady, how I could even think of stealing from such a nice person in the first place. Things were now playing on his mind. Filled with remorse at his stupid idea he headed home, the thought of robbing such a frail old lady seemed alien to his upbringing. I was never cut out for this sort of thing.

A few days later he got to thinking about just how successful his little enterprise may have been, if he hadn't had those feelings. You really need to be callous to even get involved in that way of thinking he thought.

The phone suddenly rang pulling him away from the delights of the successful haul. "Hey Mel, Sam here, are you coming down the pub, only I have a few things here you might like to see." The two of them were made redundant at the same time from the same company. "Yeah, give me ten minutes, I will be there." Mates ever since they started working together as apprentices, there was often contact between them. Sam seemed to be the successful one of the two, there wasn't much he didn't have, or couldn't afford. Mel always wondered just how well he could do whatever it was, when all he did was struggle.

The two pals sat there drinking until the moment came for Sam to produce the goods as he called them. Reaching into his inside pocket he produced a handkerchief, motioning to Mel to get closer, he then slowly opened the chewed up piece of cloth under the table.

"There you go my beauty, cast your beady eyes over that little lot!" Mel couldn't believe his eyes, there laid before him were what could only be described as the spoils from a burglary. "I got that lot from a bit of business I did the other night and it was easy, like taking candy from a baby." Mel could feel the hackles on the back of his neck rising. So this is how he does it, robbing people. And there's me thinking he was really smart, while all the time, it's just stealing other people's hard earned property.

The remorse was setting in for the second time that day. I did think of doing it myself, but I decided to forget it, you're allowed to think of things like that I suppose, but thinking about it and doing it are two different things I'm sure. Mel was by now wrestling with his conscience. Thinking about doing it is very different from doing it. I have also thought about robbing that bank up the road as well, but I didn't do that either. I will play this real cool until I find out some more information.

"Now that's very nice, a good haul, how did you manage to bring it off and all from one place, very nice indeed?" Mel nearly choked on his own words as they flowed out. Fingering the haul he could see that it was all well-worn old gold. The style was of the 1920s, necklaces, rings, a brooch and a gold Hunter style fob watch, also in the haul were two war medals.

"You can have the lot for three hundred pounds and that's my bargain price, do you want it? You'll make plenty for yourself at that price, no problem."

"If only I had some money I would go for it big time, but you know the way it is, I haven't got it and that's that." Sam was insistent. "It doesn't have to be money, I would trade it for your Mountain bike!"
"How can I trade it for my bike I wouldn't ever be

unable to get out and find a job without it?" "You won't need to work if you do it, as you're then in business in your own right. Employment problem solved at a stroke my son, got it." This was about the last thing that Mel wanted to get involved in and flatly refused.

The disappointment showed on Sam's face, he thought that Mel would be up for it. They parted company and went their separate ways. The next morning he thought long and hard about it, in some ways he would be helping a friend out and as he said. I would at least have something to do with my time. No, not my style to fence off stolen gear, what I need is full time legal employment as before, not criminal activities. Peeking through the curtains every time someone knocks the door is not way for me.

Mel's mind was made up, he was never going to risk everything for the chance of a quick buck. The torment of the next few days was unbearable, as one after another failed job applications popped through the letter box.

Mel was now wandering into the depths trying to figure out a way to get back to gainful employment. Perhaps a drink or two would clear these thoughts, not too much as I have that job interview at the Cement factory this afternoon, you never know I may be lucky this time. A sudden knock at the door brought him back to his senses. This was an unusual knock as if commanding attention.

Two Police officers stood before him, “Mr Melvyn Greenaway!”
“Yes officer, that’s right, how can I help you?”
“We have reason to believe that you were involved in a burglary in Bedford Street on the 29th, we would like you to accompany us down to the station to answer a few questions.” The thoughts of this filled him with apprehension, why would they want to talk to me?

It turned out that this was to be an informal chat and just routine, or so they said on the journey there. “We have information that on the evening of 29th you and others unknown, did break and enter the said property, what have you got to say to these charges?”
“You’ve got this all wrong, I wouldn’t do anything like that ever and it’s against my principles.”

"So could you explain how it is that your fingers prints have been found on a gold watch recovered from the proceeds?" "Oh, I know the answer to that, I was offered some jewellery in the pub at a special price. I looked it over and told the guy no thanks, not my scene."
"Who was this person?"
"I have no idea he was a stranger."
"Then could you tell us why you were caught on CCTV in Bedford Street on the day of the robbery?"

Mel knew this was the end of the line, whatever the answer they would never believe him. "I often go for a walk and sometimes along Bedford Street on my way to the pub." He was then cautioned and charged with burglary of the said property, with others unknown.

Six months had passed in that damp prison cell. He was starting to get used to the hubbub of prison life, the walls had stopped closing in on him and his cell mates had finished their sentences long ago being replaced by others of a more engaging nature. It was turning out to be more fun that he could have imagined. The three of them organised quiz nights, charades, along with the obligatory poker school, the loser would have to empty the slop bucket. Between them they were all getting on nicely and the time passed quickly.

Mel began to enjoy the company, the routine rather than getting him down was a joy to respond to each day. It was all fun, he was surprised to find himself being swallowed up in the prison system. Rather than protesting his innocence on a regular basis to anyone that would listen, he started to brag at his achievements and likened it to being a success rather than a failure.

His visitors such as they were, included Sam, the protagonist of his demise. “This is nothing to do with me Mel, I just sold the goods onto some other guy and he got caught with it. They put two and two together, then decided to pay you a visit.”

The years passed with Mel spending more and more time inside, no matter what it was he would always look forward to another few years. The regular meals, the organised regime was just up his street. No need to worry where the next meal was coming from, or the roof over his head.

The new influx of prisoners were placed around the various available cells. “Hi I’m Mel and you are?”
“Jason, call me Jase. How long have you been in then Mel?” “Ah right, now let’s see! Longer than you could ever imagine, I was totally successful and a rich man until I was caught. How about you?”
“I was framed you know, I didn’t do any of the things they charged me with.” Mel mused to himself. That reminds me of someone, way back.

Charlie and Jim both looked at each other. “Brilliant story Jack, are you trying to tell us something?”
“Yes, you will end up like Mel if you don’t mend your ways and let that be a lesson to you!”

Shortly after that little exchange I made my way back to the apartment. Barnaby was there to greet me as usual, but this time his face wasn’t its usual self and the strain was starting to show as he informed me that the police had made a visit and asked him to unlock the door to my apartment, I was furious. “You know the procedure, did they leave you a copy of their search warrant?”

"No, there arrived minutes after you went out and they were in a hurry."

"Okay, I will contact them in the next few days, now where's this package?" As he walked off to get it I noticed his unusual gait, he walked on his heels, thumping them down first and then his toes followed through as he moved forward. It reminded me of the smart looking man that propositioned Dolly that night along the riverside. He then returned with the package and a piece of folded-up paper. "You will have to sign for it." As he pushed the paper forward indicating the place for my signature .Yeah right I thought, I wonder what's written on the folded-up part. I just snatched the package and made my way to the lift as he demanded me to comply.
I was bloody mortified thinking about it all as the lift doors slowly swung open.

When I entered my apartment it was plain to see that it had been turned over very thoroughly. Everything had been searched, even the pictures on the wall had been examined. It was all getting to me. It was only when my cleaning lady Rosy opened the door with her usual words that I

started to settle down once again. "Hi Jack, are you decent?"
"Come on in Rosy, I'm decent in dress, but not in mind."
"Oh, what's the matter Jack, talk to Rosy." She then gave me one of her lingering kisses that seemed to me to be getting longer each time she visited.
"The police have just raided this apartment according to Barnaby and turned me over something rotten."

She then looked perplexed. The police haven't been here I would have noticed. I've just been cleaning in B-Block. They are the ones with those great big panoramic windows and overlook the entrance door. I would have noticed them straight away. Come on let's have a drink and a talk, I can see you need it." We were back at it again drinking and talking. It happened every time she came in just lately and a welcome break it was for me too.

She was a very shapely woman indeed and her sense of humour was along the same lines as mine, we had fun together and we knew it. That's about as far as it ever went, but there were times when she wanted a bit more than I was offering. I would always brush it off by asking her if she wanted another drink.

We were sitting out on the balcony, my only real safe place from Rosy and her amorous advances. Looking at the river current I noticed that Darren's paper aeroplane was floating past. Ah well I thought to myself, silly boy to fly in near the river then, wasn't he.

It was time to ask some pertinent questions. "Did you know that some of the girls that work on the riverside have disappeared?" I enquired.
"Yes, and I am very concerned for you and the others that have lost someone. It must be unbearable not knowing where they are. As I understand it there is only Dolly left and she said that she may have to give it all up."
I pressed her further. "Was it the same day of the week each time? I haven't looked at that yet and well I just wondered."
"Yes, all of them disappeared on a Thursday."
Snippets of information like this were slowly adding up, I drifted off in one of my thought modes. I have lots of bits of information, but not

the parts that join all of this together, slowly it was taking shape despite the missing parts.

Rosy flitted around with her feather duster thing and helped me tidy up after the burglary. Soon after she wiggled her way through my front door and was gone for another few days.

It was time to investigate the phone that Doogy found. I would at last find out surely what Charlie and Jim were up to. It was still charged up as I searched for the menu. Then to my surprise I suddenly realised that it was Sabi's phone. Complete with all texts sent and resulting return messages. I felt as if I was prying into her affairs, but it had to be done. The last text she sent was to Jane

- - - "Hi Jane, just to let you know that I have been invited to spend all night with a client, see you tomorrow. Sabi - - -

The time and day, it was a Thursday. Why didn't Jane pass the message on that Sabi left her that night? She told me that she had just disappeared and hadn't told her where she was going. That's not what it says here that's for sure. I knew that

Jane was holding out on me and there must be a reason for that, but what is it?

It was time to really get into these messages, I searched through and most of them were to various other people unknown to me and maybe just friends and acquaintances. Then a surprise one to Jane.

- - - -Hi Jane, I've been thinking about Barnaby and what you said, I would steer clear of him, he seems to have a vicious streak about him, talk to you later. Sabi - - -

So I've got it at last, Jane did want Sabi out of the flat and we know why at last, she'd got herself fixed up with that scumbag a few floors below. Well, well, who would have thought it? All we need to know now is why Jane didn't pass on the message that Sabi left. This would rattle around in my head for a few days and I knew it. What's my next move going to be, was it back to the police station, or will events take a different turn as they have today?

Time to try again

There was only one thing for it and that was to brave that police station for the second time. I didn't really want anything to do with them and it grated on my integrity to have to return. Whenever there I would often think back to when we were kids and the unwelcome look of that place, with all of its memories.

It was time to grab the bull by the horns. I did have a recent picture of Sabi and pocked it as I left the apartment that morning. It was to my advantage that I went there this time and as for the other time I visited when I dragged my feet like a spoilt school kid, this morning was different.

The same officer propped up the desk as I entered, I requested to see someone about a missing person. Then he asked my name and when I mentioned it there was a look of amusement on the officer's face. The name Sparrow had him musing to himself as he wrote it down. There was nothing amusing he could say about my name as over the years I had heard

them all.
You're all twitter and shit like a London Sparrow! Was a regular comment. He then hit me with it. "Jailbird is it?" I tried to act surprised as if I hadn't heard that one before. It was time to respond. "No, free as a bird and I intend to stay that way thank you!"

It passed the time until I was called in, to my surprise I was ushered in to see D I Trevor Watts, Charlie's brother. The last time I saw him he treated me with disdain. This time was different and how! "Nice to see you Mr Sparrow, now what can we do for you?"
"Well the last time I came in and made enquiries about my sister Sabrina going missing, you said to wait three weeks and if she hadn't returned by then to return with a recent picture and here I am, with the picture."

"Ah I see, okay fill in this missing persons form and attach the picture, then leave it with the officer at the desk on your way out."

"Is that all, my sister has been missing for weeks and you say that's all you are going to do, just leave it at the desk."

"It will be processed and our officers will have a copy. There is one other thing before you go and that's, have you seen the old tamp that gets along the riverside. An old boy with a walking stick?"

"Yes occasionally I see an old boy as you call him, pass by."

"Do you know his name by any chance and where he lives?"

I knew both the answers to that, but he wasn't going to get the information from me, so I answered. "No." He then went on asking questions. "How about Barnaby, do you know him?" This was my chance to get one up on that Barnaby. "Yes I do, he's the porter at my apartment block."

"Does he work there full time?"

"No, he has two days off a week!"

"Which days are those?" It suddenly hit me, they were including Barnaby and Doogy in their enquiries and I wondered why? Had I missed a trick? "Thursdays and Fridays." I replied.

Just one more question, has the old tramp or Barnaby given you anything just lately?" I was really stumped, Doogy gave me the phone and

Barnaby that parcel. My only chance was to answer with a question. “You should know the answer to that, didn’t you find what you were looking for in my apartment the day you raided it?”
“Sometimes these things have to be done Mr Sparrow. We have lost two items of evidence and we would like them back if possible. Namely a phone and a package have gone missing and we think you know something about them.” I just shook my head as if it was all news to me and left soon afterwards, leaving the form at the counter.

Travelling back on the bus I wondered what this was all about as I had been given both of those items in a sort of roundabout way. So it wasn’t Barnaby that had broken into my apartment as I thought all along and that lying sod Doogy hadn’t found the phone in the bushes. The police were just about an hour too early. The parcel hadn’t been collected by me and was still in the porter’s office and Doogy had only just traded the phone with me an hour earlier and it was in my pocket the day I returned to find my apartment burgled.

As I stepped down from the bus my first thoughts were for that lying little dog Doogy. I wondered if the little git was in the Riverside Café. I ordered my usual and quickly sat down in the corner so as to avoid any more of the clever talk from Brenda and to keep an eye out on the footpath below. It wasn't long before Doogy came creeping along carrying something heavy in his bag. He would be heading here, so all I had to do was wait. "Hiya Jack," he said as soon as he saw me. I replied, "How's things going mate?" Giving him the chance to sit down before I started on him.

"You're a lying little toe-rag Doogy. You told me that you found that phone under the bushes. You didn't tell me that you had nicked it off the police now did you. I have been down to the police station this morning and they said it had been stolen from them and did I know who by?"

"You didn't tell them did you Jack?"

"No, I didn't tell them that your name was Doogy Lippers and I didn't say you lived in with Mrs Jackson down by the riverside. So tell me before I ring them up and drop you in it. Where did you get the phone from and that parcel they're looking for, you thieving little dog?"

"I lifted the lot out of the back of a police car one evening, it was parked up in the back road just over there. The phone I slipped into my pocket, the parcel had your name and address on it, along with those special stamps. So I put it on the counter in the Post Office on my way past, that's all mate."

"You did well Doogy thanks for being honest, I just wondered where it came from and now I know." Brenda brought my usual over and placed it on the table. For his dishonest honesty I treated Doogy with it. I now knew that the police were involved with all of this and it was just a matter of time before I would put the final pieces of the puzzle together.

Everything today had worked out really well after the poor start. I puzzled over the package, it had those printed off stamps that the post office issue when you take something in to them and not the ordinary stick on ones. So the package must have been retrieved from the Post Office after it was posted for some reason. I now knew that the police were onto things for them to be interested. I made my way home. As I passed Barnaby I looked over and waved. To think he was my number one suspect in all of this and how wrong I had been to even blame him in the first place. In the comfort of my apartment I reminisced on some of the things that had happened in the past and the present day.

There were things to do, but in my forgetful state they just didn't get done. I stopped myself once again from sitting down and going through this little lot for the umpteenth time. It was time to lighten the load and explore the surprise package that had evaded me for so long.

The package had been delivered by the Royal Mail parcel service. I wasn't expecting anything, but it was addressed to me. Fortune favours the brave, so I quickly ripped into the outer layers of packaging. Something was different about this and it stopped me short of removing the final layers. The extra weight for what was a small package was the first thing I noticed. I investigated some more and prodded the thing in various places, it was soft and squishy. Not at all like a bottle of drink, or anything else desirable!

The smell test was up for it next and this stopped me in my tracks, it smelt like rotten meat. I then dumped the package into the freezer and hoped for the best and the best would be that it wasn't part of our family. Attached was a note made up from various newspaper and magazine clippings, stuck on at various angles with differing fonts, It was time to digest the contents of the collaged note.

"Keep your nose out of our business, or you will be next?"

The conclusion

We were still in bed together when I finished telling Rosy Brenner the story. So there you have it Rosy, that's where I was up to before it all became too much for me and as you well know, I tried to end it all. Most of it was just plain depression from trying to solve it all and getting nowhere. Rosy pressed in nearer to me as if she was trying to comfort my thoughts. "Is that when you started to make those paper aeroplanes again, taking yourself back to your childhood, were you?"

"No, I didn't make them, I fished them out of the river over the course of a few weeks. Some kid has been making them upstream from here and flying them into the river, well that's the only thing I can think of. I have seen at least six or seven float past in the last few weeks or so." Rosy reached over and picked up the paper plane that was beside me on the bedside table. She turned to me after some thought with a strange expression on her face.

"They didn't travel very far did they Jack?"
"How do you know that?"
"Well JS-112B are your initials and the number is an apartment just up the river in B-Block. I used to clean it for old Mrs Wilks before she died. Her son Barnaby is the porter here in this building. I still have the pass key in my bag and the telephone number, it's just vacant now."

I just lay there numbed by my stupidity, all of this time I had the clue right in front of me and even noticed the aircraft number and the way it was folded up. It was exactly as I had shown Sabi when we were kids. That was all of those weeks ago when I refolded Darren's paper plane. It had taken it's time, but the whole thing was starting to dawn on me at last. "Well Rosy what are we waiting for? Let's get ourselves over there and sort this thing out whatever it is."
"Hang on Jack we can't go over there until after Barnaby has left for the evening and that will be about eleven o'clock. After that we have all night to investigate."

"How about we just ring her up Rose, we have the number, worth a go isn't it?"

"No, don't do that, if that was the case then why didn't she ring you? There has to be a problem and the last thing to do is aggravate that Barnaby. He has a filthy temper and could do just about anything to her.

We need to play it extra cool for the moment and I mean cool. Let your new pal Rosy think this one out for you. You are still in shock and still not thinking correctly. We just need to give her hope and then we can relax a little."

"When we were kids we had a special ring code for the phone to let our mum know we were alright when we were away, that didn't cost anything. We didn't have any money in those days anyway. I was number two kid, so two rings."

"Now that's the way to go Jack, what was it and then she can relax knowing we are onto it all."

"Just two by two separate rings and put the phone down in between." Rosy grabbed her handbag and dialled Mrs Wilks number allowing it to ring twice and then stopped it and then did the same again shortly afterwards, stopping the call once again.

"That's the best we can do for the moment, is there anything else that you haven't told me

Jack?"
"Not that I can think of, oh Charlie and Jim will be back soon as they were only going out to place a few bets down the bookies."
"They weren't heading for the bookies when I saw them earlier they were going into B-Block! Remember when they come back not a word of this until we are sure just who is doing all of this, got it?"
"Yeah," I replied.

I was at last relieved this thing maybe coming to an end. To think that Charlie and Jim may be involved in all of this sent a shudder down my spine. I asked myself, why did they rescue me from that raging current if they are involved with the disappearances?
I was back at it again on the scenarios and I was very good at it, on many occasions I had got the whole lot wrong and ended up the creek. I will reserve judgment until things become clearer. I was being guided by Rosy who I had come to trust more than anyone else.

I suddenly thought of those packages being thrown off the railway bridge that night and the urgency in their actions, it was sending tremors of fear through my body. I hoped that they weren't packages like the one I received.

The door burst open with Charlie and Jim panting to get breath. "We've just had a race upstairs and it looks as if I've won it again," said Charlie as the two of them came to a grinding halt next to the bed.
They then spied the extra lump tucked in beside me under the covers and made silent gesticulations as to who it was. Jim mouthed silently. "Who's that?" I mouthed back. "A friend, don't ask!"
In more hushed tones. "You're supposed to be bloody recuperating you daft sod, not getting down to stuff, you must be feeling a lot better." I just nodded and cocked my head towards the door to give then a clue to make themselves scarce. I knew they would make out they didn't understand just to give me some stick. Charlie then came out with it and I felt Rosy shudder. "Do you want us to tuck you in, we can do it nicely?" Bastards I thought, they are going to milk this for all it's worth.

They did eventually leave, but not before they cupped their hands into the folds of their arms as they left with big grins spread across their faces. Rosy at last came up for air. “Have they gone Jack?”
“No, they’re still here, get down!” Rosy dived back under the covers again before she realised I was having her on. “Sod you Jack Sparrow, I should have known.”

We had waited patiently for hours until the moment was right to get ourselves over to B-Block. It was the devil’s own work for Rosy to dress me. I just about ached all over from the impact of the water, but it’s much better than being dead. These thoughts passed through my mind more than once as I struggled to get my clothes on. Walking was the next thing to master as my last bit of exercise was sort of swimming underwater. This was soon accomplished with Rosy supporting my arm.

We then headed for the door and on towards the lift, stopping occasionally for me to catch my breath. Soon the porter’s office came into view and not a moment too soon. I had to rest up a bit at this point, the chest cramps were starting to slow me down. After a while we made it to the entrance door with its extra strong return spring and squeezed ourselves through ending up out on the street.

B-Block was just across the road and was our final destination. The hard flat tarmac surface was quite a trial for me after walking on carpet. Rosy knew the entrance code and as she entered the number there was a mechanical click as the mechanism responded, we pressed the door open and were in. Now all we needed was to find the lift and push button number one that would do it. The lift swished up and when the doors opened there we were on the first floor and ready to go. Rosy had taken the liberty of another kiss on the way up just to keep me perked up. Well I suppose that's what is was for.

We soon found the door, checked the number twice 112B we repeated. It was the right number, we just stood there full of trepidation as to the end result of all of this. Rosy rooted around in her purse for the pass key, inserting it into the lock she turned the key slowly not knowing what to expect on the other side. A couple of sharp inward breaths and we slowly pushed the door open, just a little at first.

All we could hear was the phone ringing through the darkness and the smell of rotten flesh hit us just as quickly, it was the stuff of nightmares. I reached in to find the light switch. The room suddenly lit up revealing our worst fears, there were body parts left all over the place as if we had interrupted some sort of process mid-stream. Rosy let out a scream that was loud enough to wake the whole building up and was then promptly sick all over the carpet.

“You stay here Rosy and I will investigate further.” I didn’t want to do this, but of the two of us my stomach was still in the right place, but only just. I first checked the living room there was a few body parts partly wrapped up and ready it would seem for transportation to some other place.

This I hoped wasn’t what Charlie and Jim had been involved in, because if it was, they were in for a long stretch in prison. The rest of the rooms were more or less normal until it came to the bathroom.

Here I really had a grizzly surprise, the bath was completely full to overflowing with body parts draining blood.

A pair of severed woman's arms with the wrists still bound with electrical wire protruded from the pile. I then spotted a thigh with what looked like a part finished game of noughts and crosses carved into it. It was then that I realised that there were two people involved in this and I thought I knew just who they were.

A couple of large butcher's knives were lined up together laying in the hand basin, accompanied by a very sharp meat cleaver. In the corner sat an ominous looking industrial mincing machine with its motor still warm from the day's work. All the while that nuisance ringing phone added an eerie echoing sound around the place stepping up the tension.

I returned quickly to Rosy who by now had propped herself up against the door frame shaking uncontrollably and spasmodically passing out. The look on her face was that of sheer terror.

There were muffled cries from the apartment next door. "Who occupies that property?" I asked.

Rosy wasn't in a fit state to reply. I gave her a bloody good shaking and furiously asked her again. She regained her composure just enough to indicate that it was also unoccupied. "Have you got a key?"
Her eyes had a faraway look in them and she was gasping for breath. "No," she managed to splutter out." I can get one from the porter's office."
"Go and get it quick." I then pushed her in the right direction as I gesticulated to her to hurry up. I just hoped she was brave enough to return with the key.

It seemed like an age before Rosy returned, there was apprehension on her face as she passed the key over. This was something that she really didn't want to do, or be involved in. I then checked the door number off the key, it was the right one. "Do you want to be in on this Rosy, or are you happy for me to go in first?"
"You go in first please." I was still trembling as I juggled the key into the lock with my shaking hands. The door eased open, but not before squeaking loud enough to attract the neighbours. I waited a few seconds for things to settle down. A muffled sound was coming from inside. Reaching

in feeling for the light switch, at last I managed to switch it on.

Everything thing about the apartment looked normal. Rosy by now was starting to get interested and slowly followed me in holding onto the back of my jacket. Every time we whispered to each other it was responded to by a muffled response. Slowly investigating the rest of the rooms proved to be fruitless. The bathroom door had what looked like a recently installed heavy duty padlock fitted to the outside. I decided to knock gently for a response. There was a muffled reply each time I tried.

"Right Rosy, what have we got to get that padlock off?" Rosy was stumped on this one until she remembered her fire drill. "Just outside in the passage way where the lift stops there is a fire axe in a glass case hanging on the wall."
"Go and get it." Rosy soon returned with an enormous two handed axe. "Close the front door we don't want to wake the whole building up."

The axe was much too heavy for me. "I can't lift that thing on my own Rosy you will have to give me a hand." We both struggled to keep the axe lined up on the padlock as we continually hacked away at it. Very slowly we were making headway as the hasp buckled. After many attempts with a few of them glancing off the door frame we eventually had the lock dangling on its hasp. My chest pains were even worse by now as I could barely turn the door handle.

I pushed the door open and in the half-light that was emanating from the hallway, I could see Sabi tied up and gagged. We both tore at her bindings until she lay there free at last. There were no words from us as we group hugged for what seemed ages. She was severely underweight and emaciated. The ambulance arrived about twenty minutes later, followed by the police. Sabi was taken away and at last she was in good hands.

It was all over, or so the police thought, until the two of us unlocked 112B and showed the police just what we had discovered. Barnaby and his stand in friend Simon were arrested soon after. The police took the stinking package from my freezer which tuned out to be Simon's dead cat. They had tried to warn me off, but in their panic to get rid of me they had only made me more inquisitive. Rosy was the one that had spotted the aircraft markings, none, of it was down to me.

Now we come to those mates of mine, Mad Charlie and Jim. They had saved me from that raging current, only for me to nearly drop them in serious trouble with my persistent enquiries. Unbeknown to me they had rented the apartment right next door to where we found Sabi and set up a cannabis factory complete with full hydroponics. Things were going very well until through me the police became interested in the disappearances. This resulted in them dumping the incriminating evidence off the railway bridge that night as they panicked to absolve themselves from any involvement. Their main outlet was the local prison as they had a few contacts with the boys in blue.

Charlie and Jim still come round for a free drink from time to time. I did ask them once if the factory was still going over in B-Block. To which they answered, “Mind your own bloody business.” Rosy moved in with me and we got ourselves together at last. If it hadn’t been for Rosy then this case may never have been solved. It was due mainly to her straight forward observation that we entered-B-Block that fateful night. I do occasionally hear the words. “Let’s get married and make this thing legal!” Being a single man for so long, it would take a lot more than a few words to convince me. Charlie and Jim said they would like to be my bridesmaids, that’s the sort of thing I had to put up with from them at times. I often thought I might give it ago just to see those two dressed up for a change.

The culprits were all given long prison sentences. Barnaby and Simon received two life sentences with no chance of a parole board review for twenty years. Jane was given two years for aiding and abetting, along with concealing evidence. She apparently had a dislike towards working girls and had helped things along. The police had their first suspicions about Barnaby and Simon when the Post Office refused to deliver the package. It had managed to get through in the end as Doogy had put it back on the counter along with the rest of the completed post. Doogy it turned out was just a thieving little git, well we all knew that anyway.

Sabi recovered and she now works at the gentle art of flower arranging and has decided to give up her life as a part-time working girl. She had dropped her phone that night when she realised that she was about to be kidnapped. It turned out in the end that Sheila and Caroline were the first to go and Sabi was to be next. Sabi had understood the telephone ring code and said it was the best sound she had ever heard.

Her saving grace was the exercise book and pencil they had left her, along with the fact that she had remembered how to fold up that paper plane.

www.ingramcontent.com/pod-product-compliance
Ingram Content Group UK Ltd.
Pitfield, Milton Keynes, MK11 3LW, UK
UKHW021050270726
13967UKWH00012B/194